yellow crayon this page 1/09 By.

APR 0 8 2009	DATE DUE NOV 2008
APR 2 5 2009	DEC 0 8 2008
FEB 1 7 2011	
NOV 0 8 2012	JAN 09
	NOV 2 8 2010

Kindness

Kimberley Jane Pryor

 **Marshall Cavendish**
Benchmark
New York

This edition first published in 2009 in the United States of America by Marshall Cavendish Benchmark.

Marshall Cavendish Benchmark
99 White Plains Road
Tarrytown, NY 10591
www.marshallcavendish.us

First published in 2008 by
MACMILLAN EDUCATION AUSTRALIA PTY LTD
15–19 Claremont St, South Yarra 3141

Visit our Web site at www.macmillan.com.au or go directly to www.macmillanlibrary.com.au

Associated companies and representatives throughout the world.

Library of Congress Cataloging-in-Publication Data

Pryor, Kimberley Jane.
    Kindness / by Kimberley Jane Pryor.
        p. cm. — (Values)
    Includes index.
    ISBN 978-0-7614-3126-8
    1. Kindness—Juvenile literature. 2. Children—Conduct of life—Juvenile literature. I. Title.
    BJ1533.K5P79 2008
177'.7—dc22

                                                        2008001661

Edited by Helena Newton
Text and cover design by Christine Deering
Page layout by Raul Diche and Domenic Lauricella
Photo research by Naomi Parker and Legend Images

Printed in the United States

Acknowledgments
The author and the publisher are grateful to the following for permission to reproduce copyright material:

Front cover photograph of brother and sister reading together © oleg filipchuk/iStockphoto.com

Photos courtesy of:
BananaStock, 7; © Elenathewise/Dreamstime.com, 17; MIXA/Getty Images, 5; Photodisc/Getty Images, 21, 26, 27; © Franky De Meyer/iStockphoto.com, 12; © Jaimie Duplass/iStockphoto.com, 24, 29; © oleg filipchuk/iStockphoto.com, 1, 10; © Eileen Hart/iStockphoto.com, 16; © Aman Khan/iStockphoto.com, 6; © manxman/iStockphoto.com, 25; © marmion/iStockphoto.com, 3, 9, 15; © Carmen Martinez Banús/iStockphoto.com, 13; © pamspix/iStockphoto.com, 28; © Cheryl Paquin/iStockphoto.com, 23; © Oleg Prikhodko/iStockphoto.com, 30; © sonyae/iStockphoto.com, 22; © Karen Struthers/iStockphoto.com, 20; © Marzanna Syncerz/iStockphoto.com, 4 © Simone van den Berg/iStockphoto.com, 11; Photodisc, 14; Paul Burns/Photolibrary.com RF, 8; Photos.com, 18, 19.

While every care has been taken to trace and acknowledge copyright, the publisher tenders their apologies for any accidental infringement where copyright has proved untraceable. Where the attempt has been unsuccessful, the publisher welcomes information that would redress the situation.

For Nick, Ashley and Thomas

1 3 5 6 4 2

Contents

Glossary words

When a word is printed in **bold**, you can look up its meaning in the Glossary on page 31.

Values

Values are the things you believe in. They guide the way:

- you think
- you speak
- you **behave**

Values help you to play fairly with your friends on climbing equipment.

Values help you to decide what is right and what is wrong. They also help you to live your life in a **meaningful** way.

Following the rules of a jump rope game makes the game fun for everyone.

Kindness

Kindness is being friendly. It is smiling at other people and speaking in a friendly voice.

A happy face looks friendly.

Kindness is also noticing when other people are sad, hurt, or in trouble. It is feeling that you would like to help them.

It would be kind to help someone who cannot reach a high shelf.

7

Kind People

Kind people are **thoughtful** toward others. They think of nice things to do for others and enjoy making people feel special.

Visiting a friend in hospital may cheer her up.

Kind people are interested in other people. They care about their family, friends, and neighbors.

Older people have interesting stories to tell younger people.

Being Kind to Family

Kind people care about the members of their family. They enjoy talking to them, eating with them, and playing with them.

Reading a story to a younger family member shows kindness.

It is kind to do nice things for the people in your family. This shows how much you love them.

Giving a flower to someone makes them feel special.

Being Kind to Friends

Kind people share things with their friends. They trust their friends to look after their special toys.

It is fun to share a dollhouse with a friend.

You can show kindness by taking turns with your friends. Sometimes you can choose a game to play. Sometimes you can let your friends choose a game to play.

Taking turns to choose a game means everybody gets to play his or her favorite game.

Being Kind to Neighbors

Kind people help their neighbors. When their neighbors are away on vacation, they do jobs for them. They might feed their neighbors' pets, water their plants, or collect their mail.

While your neighbors are away, you can help by watering their flowers.

Kind people do kind things for people in their neighborhood. They help people in need. They may give unwanted magazines and books to local schools and hospitals.

Old magazines are very useful for school craft projects.

Ways To Be Kind

There are many different ways to be kind to your family, friends, and neighbors. Being friendly is a good way to start being kind.

Waving is a friendly sign for hello and goodbye.

Being **generous** and helpful are other good ways to practice kindness. Feeling **sympathy** for other people and being ready to help them is also kind.

You may ask to walk the dog of a friend or neighbor to help them out.

Being Friendly

Being friendly is one way to be kind. You look friendly when you smile because your smile shows others that you like them.

A smile can make a visitor feel welcome.

It is friendly to say "hello" to the people who help at your school. This lets them know that you **appreciate** the work they do.

People who help at your school like to see friendly faces.

Being Generous

Being generous is another way to show kindness. Some people are very generous and they share what they have with others.

It is generous to share your special felt pens and crayons with a friend.

Generous people give away outgrown clothes and toys. They know that these things will be valued by others. They give them to friends who need them, or to **nonprofit thrift stores**.

Nonprofit thrift stores raise money for people in need by selling secondhand clothes.

Helping Others

Helping others is a kind thing to do. It is helpful when you do things that need to be done, without being asked.

Carrying groceries at the supermarket can be very helpful.

Everyone needs help sometimes. Some older people need help with housework and gardening.

You can help by raking leaves in an older person's yard.

Helping People in Need

It is kind to help people in need in your neighborhood. Families may be in need because of sickness or lack of money. They may need help with meals.

It is kind to make food for a family in need.

Some people **sponsor** children in need. The money they send provides food, clean drinking water, and health care.

In Afghanistan, many people have to walk a long way to get fresh water from a well.

Feeling Sympathy

Feeling sympathy for others is part of kindness. When someone is sad, hurt, or in trouble, it is kind to give them **support**.

Comforting a friend who is sad shows sympathy.

You can support others by comforting them or helping them. This shows them that you care.

A neighbor who has fallen off her bike may need your help.

Caring

Kind people care for their pets. When they get a new pet, they find out what it needs. Then they give it the right things, such as food and water.

When you look after pet guinea pigs, you need to feed them special food.

Kind people care about the environment. They put their garbage in garbage cans. This stops it from becoming litter. Litter makes the environment dirty and may hurt animals.

People who care about the environment put their garbage in the can.

Personal Set of Values

There are many different values. Everyone has a personal set of values. This set of values guides people in big and little ways in their daily lives.

Vets are usually very kind to animals.

Glossary

appreciate   are grateful for

behave   act in a certain way

generous   willing to give what you have to other people

meaningful   important or valuable

nonprofit thrift stores   stores that sell secondhand goods to raise money for people in need

sponsor   help a person or a group of people by giving them money; the person who gives this help is also called a sponsor

support   help or comfort

sympathy   the feeling you have when you are sorry for someone who is sad, ill, or in trouble

thoughtful   showing that you think and care about others

Index